Plate 1 Pendean Farmhouse before dismantling. (National Monuments Record, Royal Commission on Historical Monuments, London.)

Plate 2 Pendean Farmhouse as re-erected at Weald and Downland Open Air Museum, Singleton, Sussex. Late sixteenth-century farmhouse. (Photograph taken from the opposite direction from Plate 1.) (Photo: Judges Limited, Hastings.)

Plate 3 Cottage in Station Road, Coningsby, Lincolnshire. Early seventeenth century, timber frame with mud infill. (National Monuments Record, Royal Commission on Historical Monuments, London.)

Plate 4 Westwood Farm, Corfe Castle, Dorset. Early seventeenth century. (National Monuments Record, Royal Commission on Historical Monuments, London.)

Plate 5   Scotland Farm, Corfe Castle, Dorset. Dated 1665. The extension to the left was added later. (National Monuments Record, Royal Commission on Historical Monuments, London.)

Plate 6   Merton Manor Farm, Gamlingay, Cambridgeshire, viewed from the south east. Late sixteenth century with substantial alterations and East wing added around 1600. (National Monuments Record, Royal Commission on Historical Monuments, London.)

Plate 7 East Farm, Piddlehinton, Dorset. Dated 1622, though part to the left was added later in the seventeenth century. (National Monuments Record, Royal Commission on Historical Monuments, London.)

Plate 8 Sanders, Lettaford, Devon. Early seventeenth century. Long-house with byre at the lower end. (Photograph by courtesy of Devon County Council.)

Plate 9 Outbuilding for farm labourer at Hall Farm, Sustead, Norfolk. Farmhand lived in the right-hand side, note the elaborate chimney (early seventeenth century). The use of brick at this date is explained by the fact that it was one of a number of outbuildings attached to the hall, therefore it is not strictly vernacular. (National Monuments Record, Royal Commission on Historical Monuments, London.)

Plate 10 Newhouse Farm, Bishopdale, Yorkshire, viewed from the north east. Dated 1635. (National Monuments Record, Royal Commission on Historical Monuments, London.)

Plate 11   Tudor House, Exeter c. 1600. (Photograph courtesy of Devon County Council.)

Plate 12   Feathers Inn, Ludlow, Shropshire 1603. (National Monuments Record, Royal Commission on Historical Monuments, London.)

Plate 13   The parlour, Feathers Inn, Ludlow. (National Monuments Record, Royal Commission on Historical Monuments, London.)

Plate 14   Haunt Hill House, Weldon, Northamptonshire. Dated 1636, 1647. Side elevation.
The home of a master-builder with elaborate ornament clearly advertising his trade and skill.
(National Monuments Record, Royal Commission on Historical Monuments, London.)

Plate 15   Haunt Hill House, Weldon, Northamptonshire. Front view. (National Monuments
Record, Royal Commission on Historical Monuments, London.)

Plate 16   Sparrowe's House,
Ipswich, Suffolk c. 1670, with
plasterwork decoration.
(National Monuments Record,
Royal Commission on
Historical Monuments,
London.)

Plate 17   The oak room
(early seventeenth century),
Sparrowe's House, Ipswich.
(National Monuments Record,
Royal Commission on Historical
Monuments, London.)

Plate 18   Tomson Farm, Anderson, Dorset. Early seventeenth century, porch extension later. (National Monuments Record, Royal Commission on Historical Monuments, London.)

Plate 19 Anderson Manor, Dorset 1622; side extension added in late seventeenth century. (National Monuments Record, Royal Commission on Historical Monuments, London.)

Plate 20 Raynham Hall (East Front), Norfolk c. 1635. Designed by Sir Roger Townsend probably with assistance from Inigo Jones. (Photograph by A. F. Kersting.)

Plate 21 Designs for the front elevation of the Prince's Lodging, Newmarket, Cambridgeshire, by Inigo Jones (c. 1618). The lower design probably represents the building as completed. (Reproduced by courtesy of the Drawings Collection, British Architectural Library, Royal Institute of British Architects, London.)

Plate 22 Inigo Jones, the Queen's House, Greenwich (1616–35), the South Front. The side colonnades were added later. (National Monuments Record, Royal Commission on Historical Monuments, London.)

Plate 23   Queen Anne of Denmark by Paul van Somer, 1617. (Copyright Reserved. Reproduced by gracious permission of Her Majesty the Queen.)

Plate 24   Thomas, Earl of Arundel, by Daniel Mytens c. 1618. (National Portrait Gallery on deposit at Arundel Castle. Photograph by courtesy of the Courtauld Institute, University of London.)

Plate 25 Penshurst Place, Kent, fourteenth-century parts to the right, sixteenth-century wing to left, added later. (Country Life photograph.)

Plate 26 Penshurst Place, Kent, Great Hall. Mid-fourteenth century, screen early seventeenth century. (Photograph Country Life *by permission of Viscount De L'Isle, VC, KG.)*

Plate 27 Audley End, Saffron Walden, Cambridgeshire, completed 1616. The front two courtyards were demolished in the eighteenth century. (Reproduced from Henry Winstanley, The Royal Palace of Audley End, 1688, by permission of the British Library Board.)

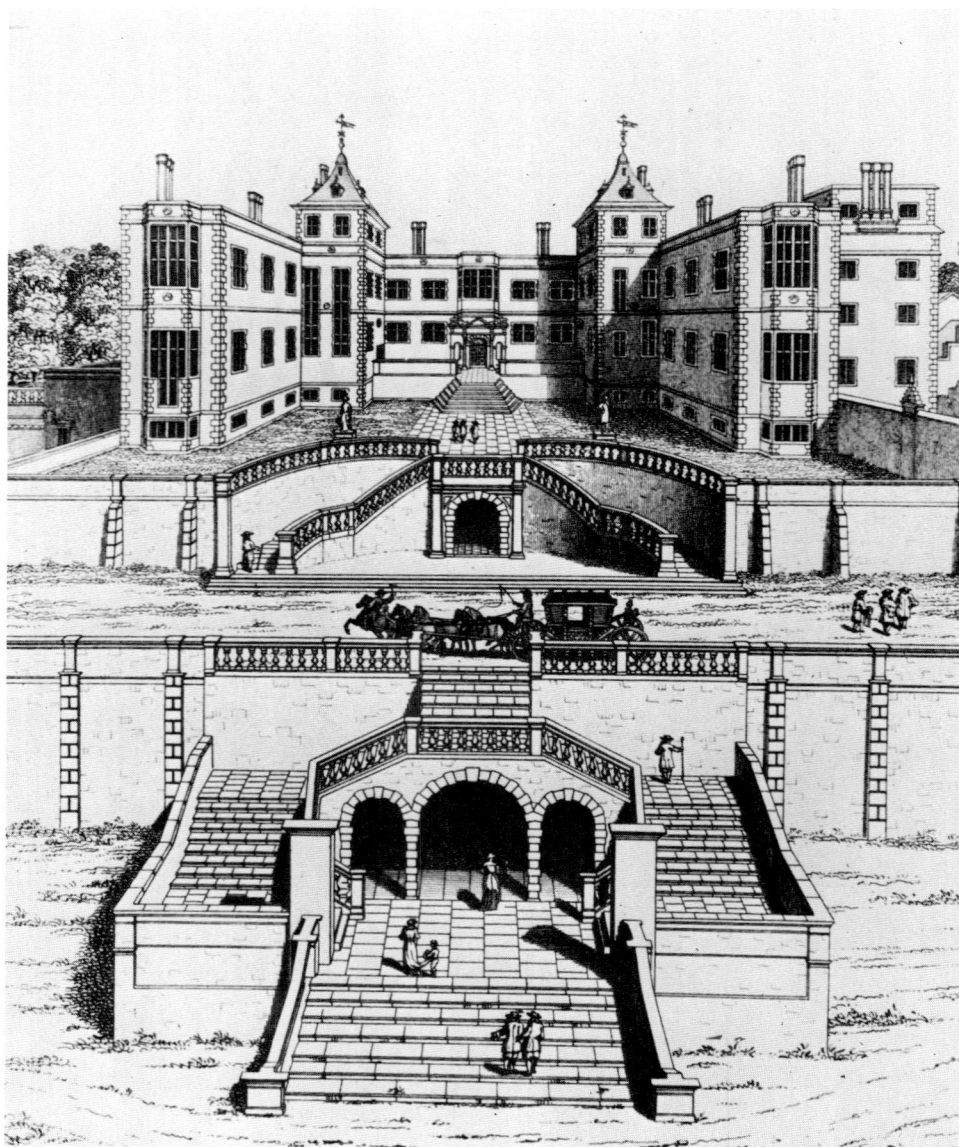

Plate 28 Wimbledon House, Surrey. Begun in 1588 it was demolished in the eighteenth century. Engraved by Henry Winstanley. (Mansell Collection.)

Plate 29 *Hatfield House, Hertfordshire, 1611. The King's Lodgings were to the right, Lord Salisbury's were below, and the Queen's Lodgings were to the left. The central loggia and gate-house were designed by Inigo Jones. The view is of the South Front. (Photograph by A. F. Kersting.)*

Plate 30 Hatfield House, Hertfordshire. The grand staircase, designed and executed by the master carpenter Robert Lyninge, who was also responsible for the overall design of the house. (National Monuments Record, Royal Commission on Historical Monuments, London.)

Plate 31 Hatfield House, Hertfordshire. The long gallery. (National Monuments Record, Royal Commission on Historical Monuments, London.)

Plate 32 Knole House, Sevenoaks, Kent. Great hall c. 1610. (Country Life photograph by courtesy of the National Trust.)

Plate 33   Inigo Jones, Queen's Chapel, St James's. Exterior. (Photograph by A. F. Kersting.)

Plate 34   Inigo Jones, Queen's Chapel, St James's. Interior. (Photograph by A. F. Kersting.)

Plate 35   Triumphal arch erected at the time of the coronation of James I, from Stephen Harrison (1640) The Arches of Triumph erected in honour of the High and Mighty Prince James I ... at his Entrance and passage through ... London upon the 15th day of March 1603. *(Reproduced by permission of the British Library Board.)*

*Plate 36   Triumphal arch erected at the time of the coronation of James I, from Stephen Harrison
(1640)* The Arches of Triumph erected in honour of the High and Mighty Prince
James I . . . at his Entrance and passage through . . . London upon the 15th day of
March 1603. *(Reproduced by permission of the British Library Board.)*

Plate 37   Inigo Jones, design for King James I's catafalque at Westminster Abbey. (Reproduced by kind permission of the Provost and Fellows of Worcester College, Oxford. Photograph by courtesy of the Courtauld Institute of Art, University of London.)

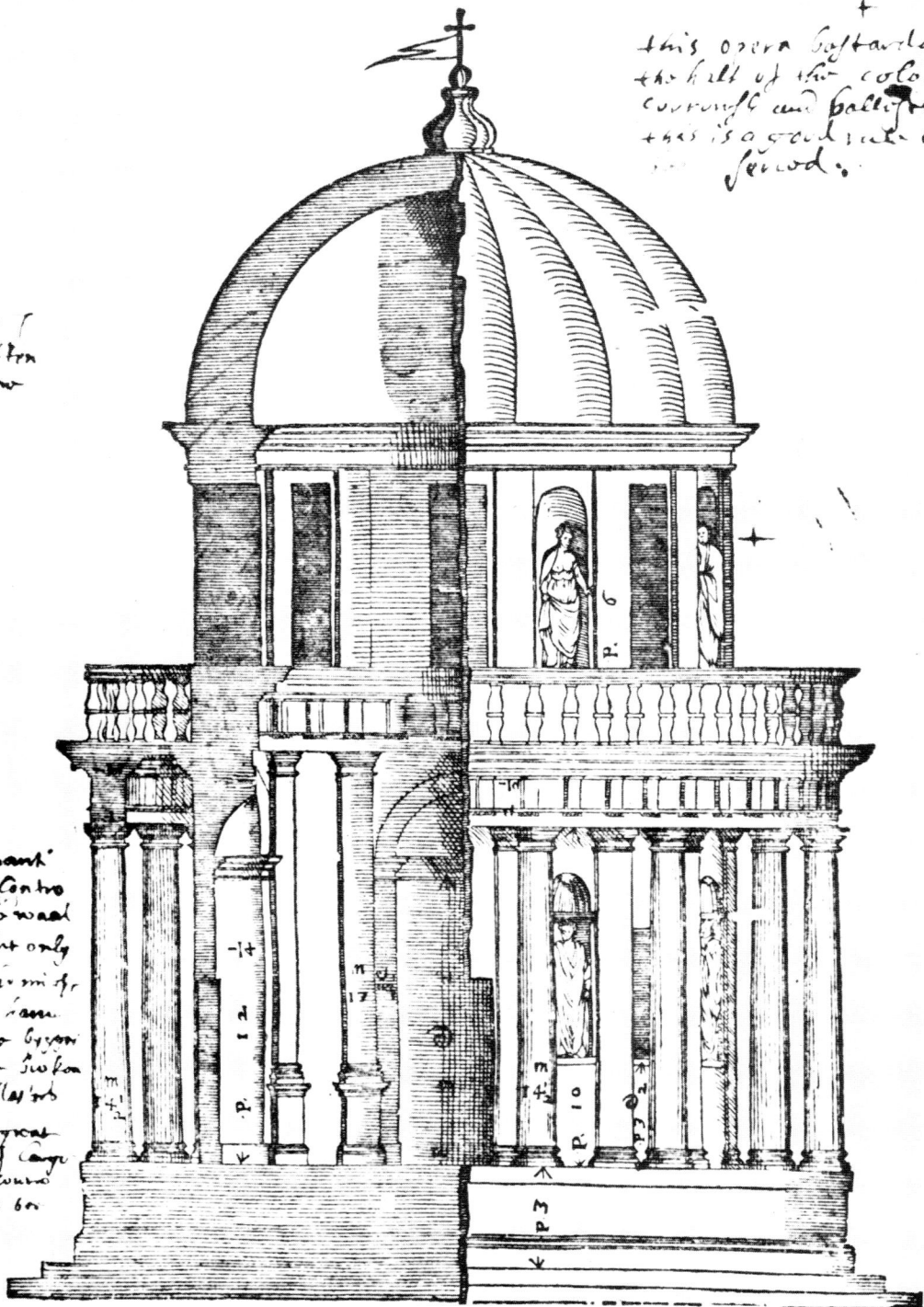

Plate 38   Bramante, Tempietto, San Pietro in Montorio 1502, reproduced from Inigo Jones's copy of Palladio's Four Books of Architecture, *1601 edition, p 66. (Reproduced from the facsimile published by Oriel Press, 1970, by kind permission of the Provost and Fellows of Worcester College, Oxford.)*

Plate 39   Inigo Jones, design for a Triumphal Arch, Temple Bar, London. (Reproduced by courtesy of the Drawings Collection, British Architectural Library, Royal Institute of British Architects, London.)

Plates 40 and 41   Detailed drawings by John Webb from Inigo Jones's Temple Bar Triumphal Arch design. (Reproduced by courtesy of the Drawings Collection, British Architectural Library, Royal Institute of British Architects, London.)

Plate 42   Inigo Jones, costume design for Berenice in The Masque of Queens, *1609. (Devon-shire Collections, Chatsworth, reproduced by permission of the Trustees of the Chatsworth Settlement from a photograph provided by the Courtauld Institute of Art, University of London.)*

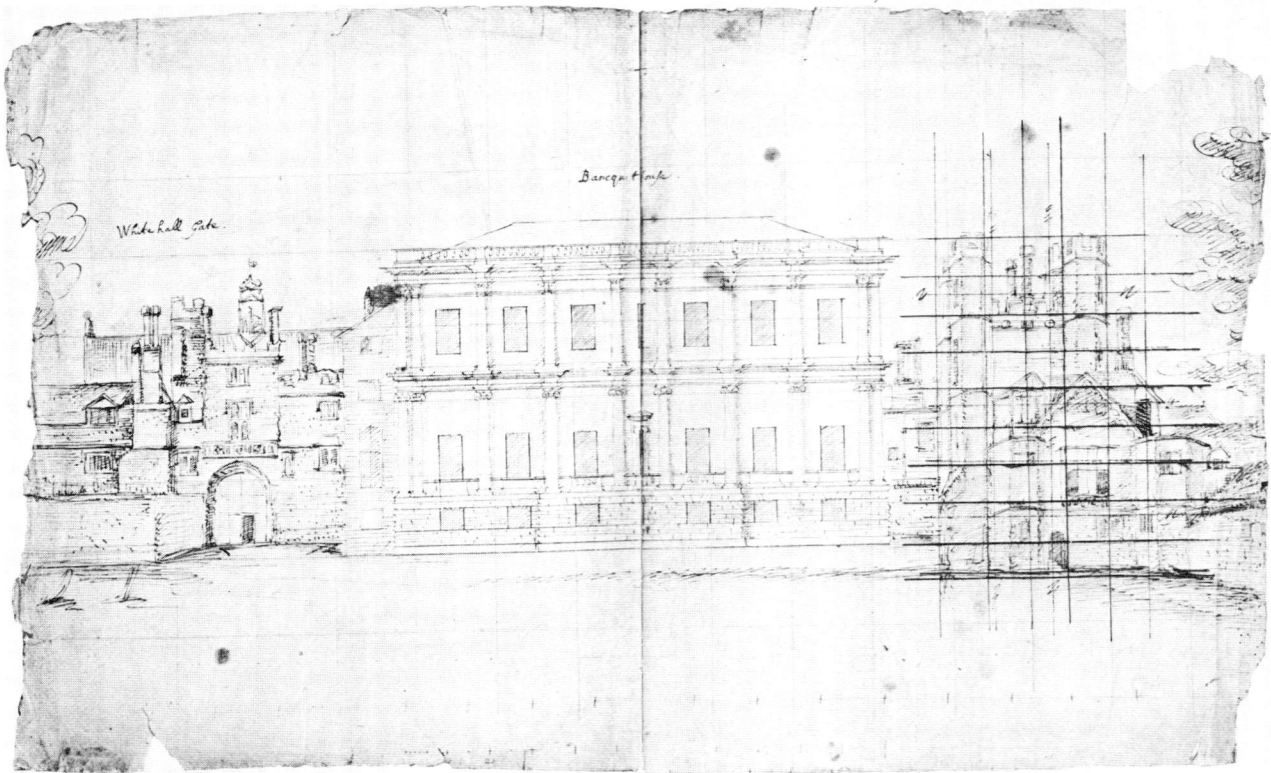

Plate 43   Inigo Jones, 'Whitehall Banqueting House', a design for scene 1 of Time Vindicated to Himself and to His Honours, *1623. (Private Collection.)*

Plate 44   Inigo Jones, 'A Roman Forum', a design for scene 1 of Albion's Triumph, *1631. (Devonshire Collections, Chatsworth, reproduced by permission of the Trustees of the Chatsworth Settlement from a photograph provided by the Courtauld Institute of Art, University of London.)*

Plate 45   Inigo Jones, 'A Peaceful Country', a design for scene 2 of Salmacida Spolia, 1640.
(Devonshire Collections, Chatsworth, reproduced by permission of the Trustees of the Chatsworth
Settlement from a photograph provided by the Courtauld Institute of Art, University of London.)

Plate 46   Inigo Jones, 'Suburbs of a Great City', a design for scene 4 of Salmacida Spolia, 1640.
(Devonshire Collections, Chatsworth, reproduced by permission of the Trustees of the Chatsworth
Settlement from a photograph provided by the Courtauld Institute of Art, University of London.)

Plate 47   Inigo Jones, 'Design for the newe Italyan Gate', Arundel House, London. (Reproduced by courtesy of the Drawings Collection, British Architectural Library, Royal Institute of British Architects, London.)

Plate 48   John Smythson, elevation of 'the newe Italyan gate', 1618–19. (Smythson Collection (20) 1, reproduced by courtesy of the Drawings Collection, British Architectural Library, Royal Institute of British Architects, London.)

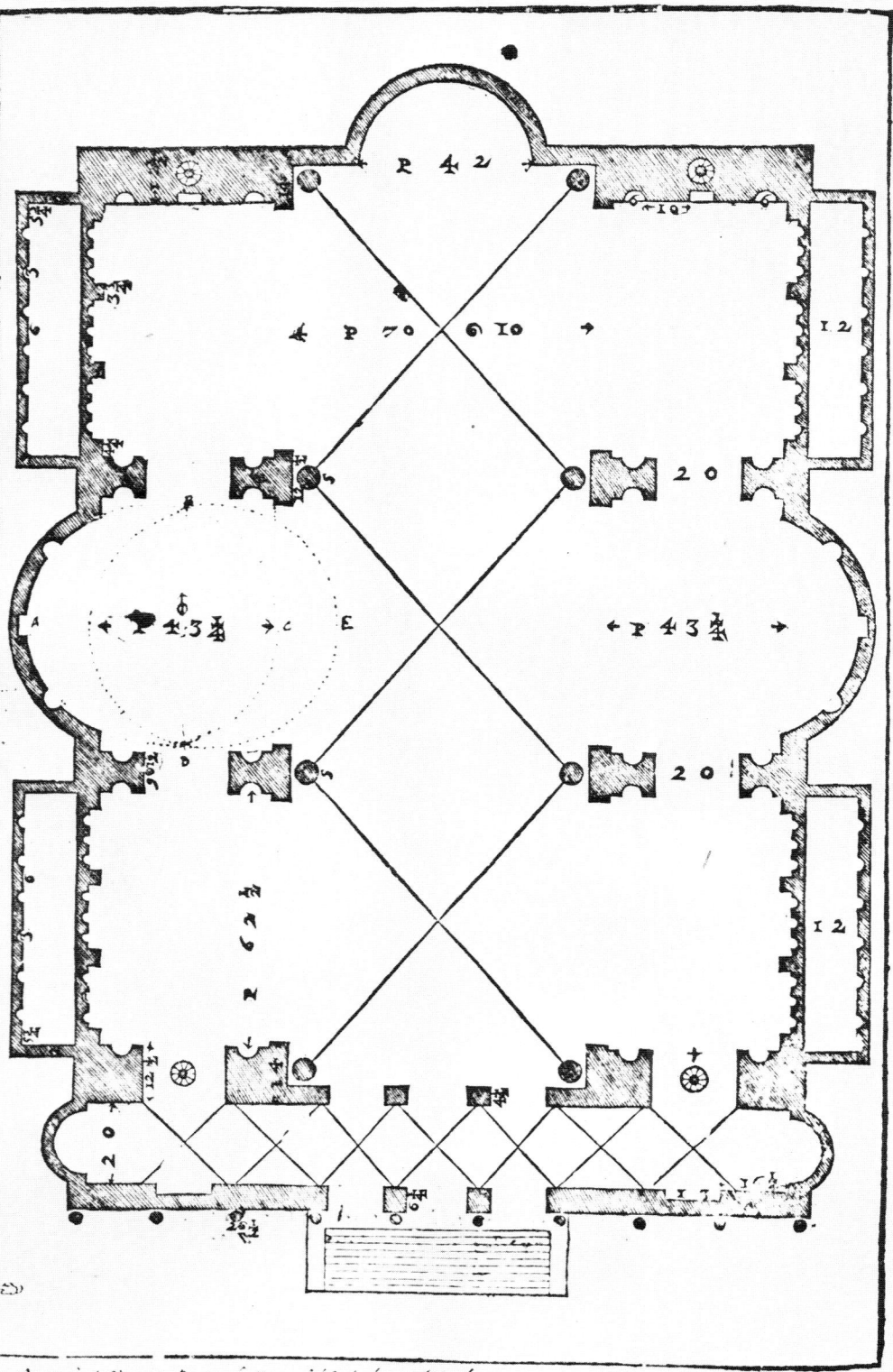

Plate 49   Andrea Palladio, 'Temple of Peace' (Basilica of Maxentius), reproduced from Inigo Jones's copy of Four Books of Architecture, 1601 edition, Book IV, p 12, plan. (Reproduced from the facsimile published by Oriel Press, 1970, by kind permission of the Provost and Fellows of Worcester College, Oxford.)

Plate 50   Andrea Palladio, 'Temple of Peace' (Basilica of Maxentius), reproduced from Inigo Jones's copy of Four Books of Architecture, 1601 edition, Book IV, p 13, elevation and section. (Reproduced from the facsimile published by Oriel Press, 1970, by kind permission of the Provost and Fellows of Worcester College, Oxford.)

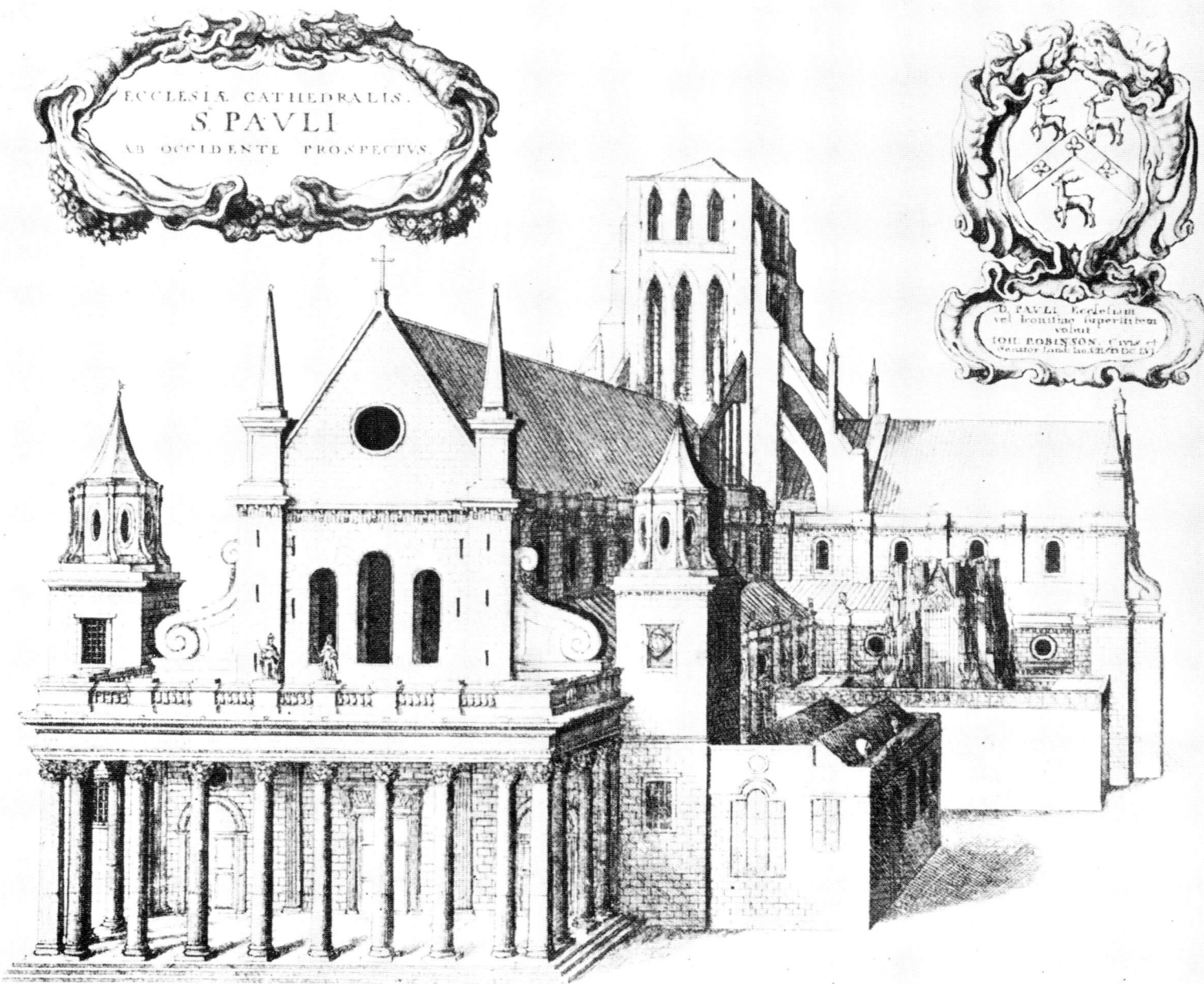

Plate 51   Wenceslas Hollar, sketch of Inigo Jones's west portico, old St Paul's, London 1634–5.
(Private Collection.)

Plate 52   Andrea Palladio, 'Temple of the Sun and Moon', reproduced from Inigo Jones's copy of Four Books of Architecture, *1601 edition, Book IV, p 36. (Reproduced from the facsimile published by Oriel Press, 1970, by kind permission of the Provost and Fellows of Worcester College, Oxford.)*

Plate 53   *John Webb, after Inigo Jones, elevation of flank of Star Chamber project, 1617. (Reproduced by kind permission of the Provost and Fellows of Worcester College, Oxford. Photograph by courtesy of the Courtauld Institute of Art, University of London.)*

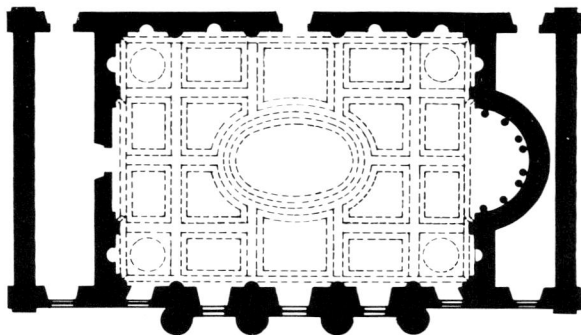

Plate 54   *Plan of Star Chamber project, 1617. (Plan from John Summerson (1966)* Inigo Jones, *Harmondsworth, Penguin Books by permission of the publishers.)*

Plate 55 John Webb, for Inigo Jones, section of Star Chamber project, 1617. (Reproduced by kind permission of the Provost and Fellows of Worcester College, Oxford. Photograph by courtesy of the Courtauld Institute, University of London.)

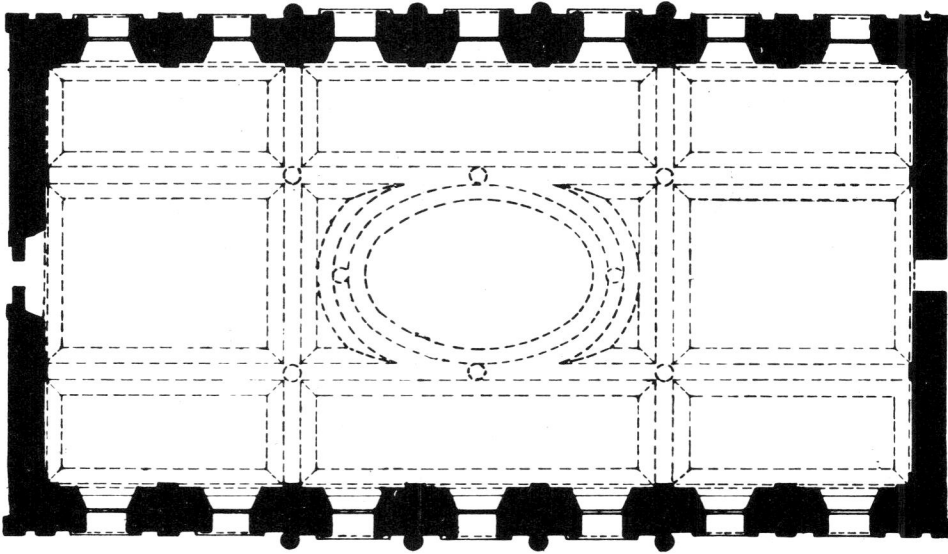

Plate 56   Inigo Jones, Banqueting House, Whitehall, plan, 1619–22. (Plan from John Summerson (1966) Inigo Jones, Harmondsworth, Penguin Books by permission of the publishers.)

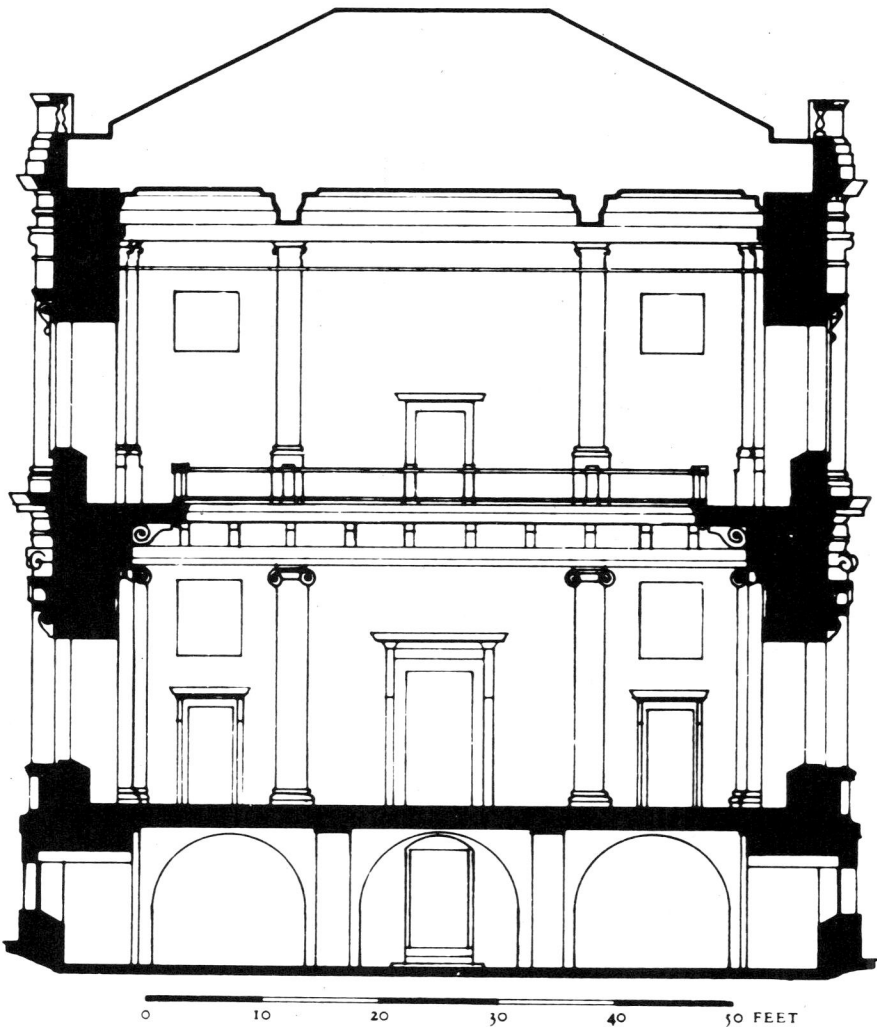

0   10   20   30   40   50 FEET

Plate 57   Inigo Jones, Banqueting House, Whitehall, section, 1619–22. (Plan from John Summerson (1966) Inigo Jones, Harmondsworth, Penguin Books by permission of the publishers.)

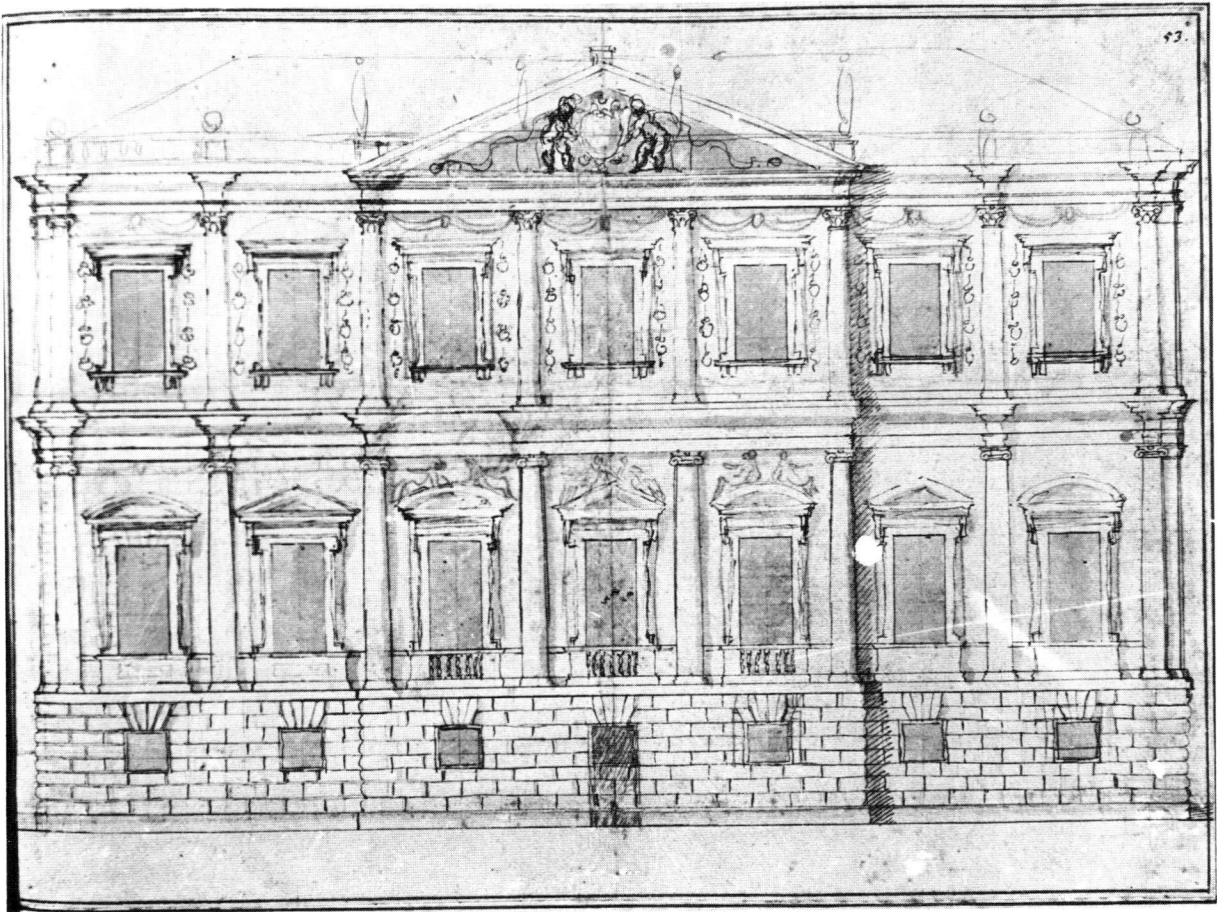

Plate 58   Inigo Jones, preliminary elevation for the main façade of the Banqueting House, 1619. (Devonshire Collections, Chatsworth, reproduced by permission of the Trustees of the Chatsworth Settlement from a photograph provided by the Courtauld Institute of Art, University of London.)

Plate 59   Inigo Jones, Banqueting House, exterior. (Photograph by A. F. Kersting.)

Plate 60   Inigo Jones, Banqueting House, interior from the gallery. (Photograph by A. F. Kersting.)

Plate 61   Contemporary print of the execution of Charles I, 30 January 1649. (E. Gardner Collection, reproduced in Walter Besant (1903) London in the time of the Stuarts, London, A & C Black.)

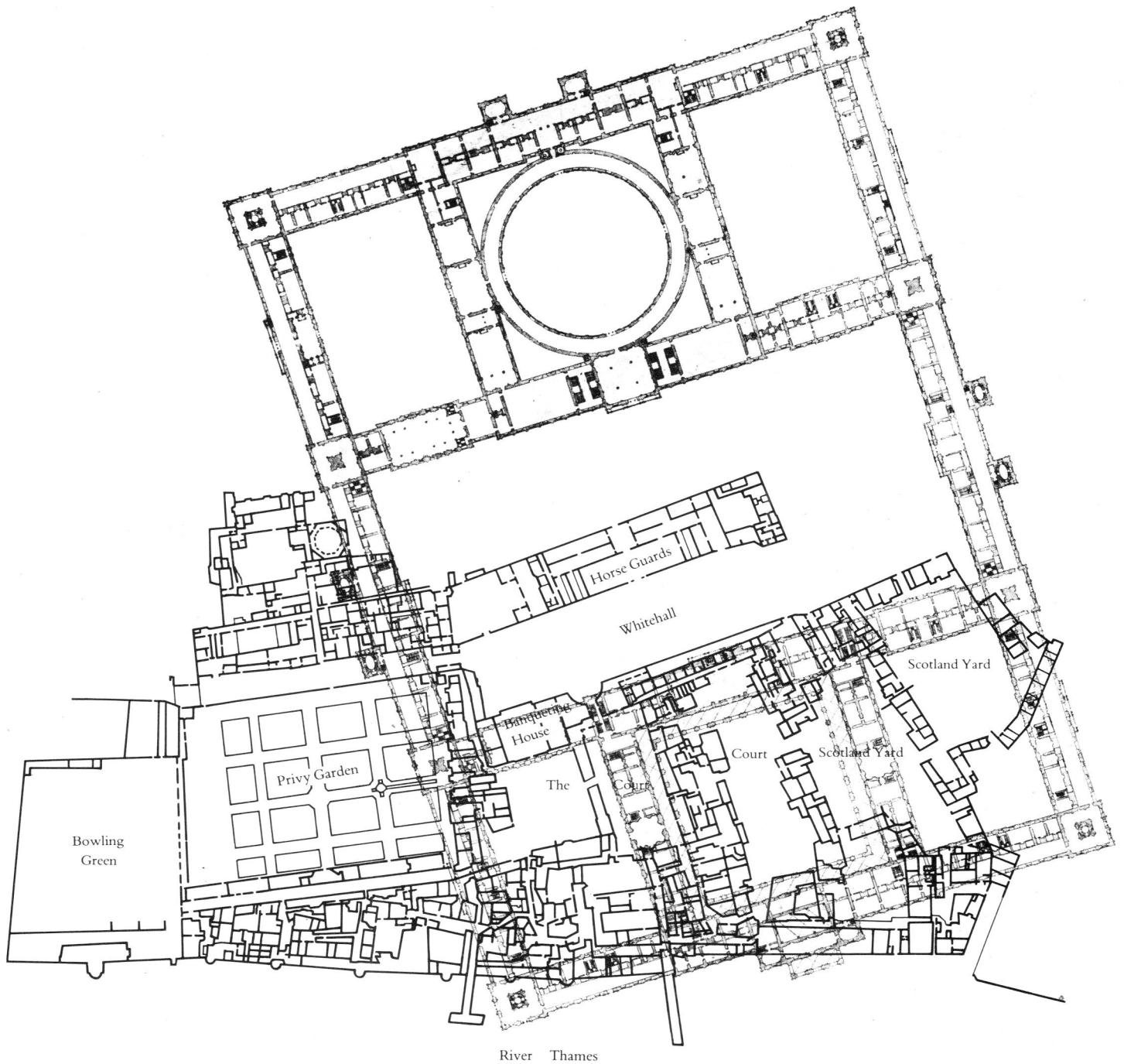

Plate 62 *Survey plan of Whitehall Palace c. 1638 combined with outline of Webb's 'K'*
project for Whitehall Palace, 1638–47. (Survey plan reproduced by permission of the Society of
Antiquaries, London. 'K' plan reproduced by kind permission of the Provost and Fellows of
Worcester College, Oxford from a photograph provided by the Courtauld Institute of Art,
University of London.)

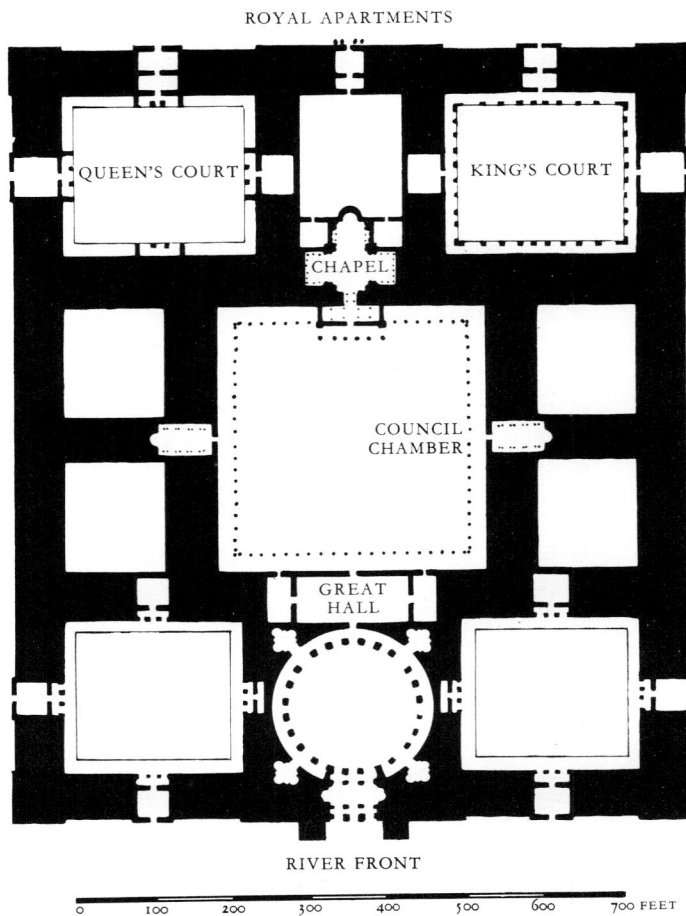

Plate 63 Inigo Jones and John Webb, 'Preliminary' project for the new Whitehall Palace in St James's Park, c. 1638. (Plan from John Summerson (1966) Inigo Jones, Harmondsworth, Penguin Books by permission of the publishers.)

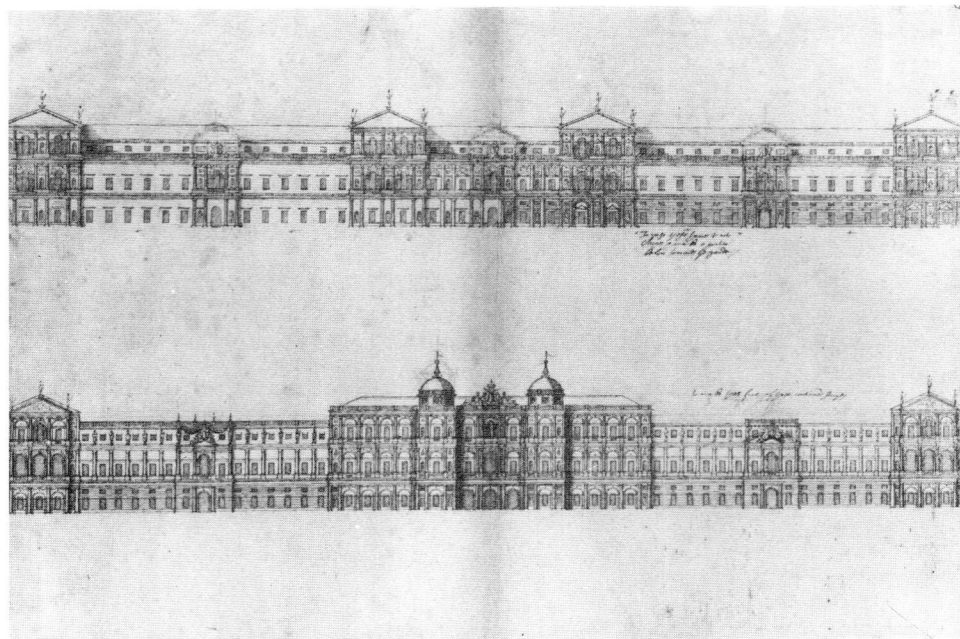

Plate 64 John Webb's elevations of Park Front and River Front of 'Preliminary' project for the new Whitehall Palace in St James's Park, c. 1638. (Reproduced by kind permission of the Provost and Fellows of Worcester College, Oxford. Photograph by courtesy of the Courtauld Institute of Art, University of London.)

Plate 65   Pedro Machuca, Circular Court, Alhambra, 1526. (Ampliacones y Reproducciones MAS, Barcelona.)

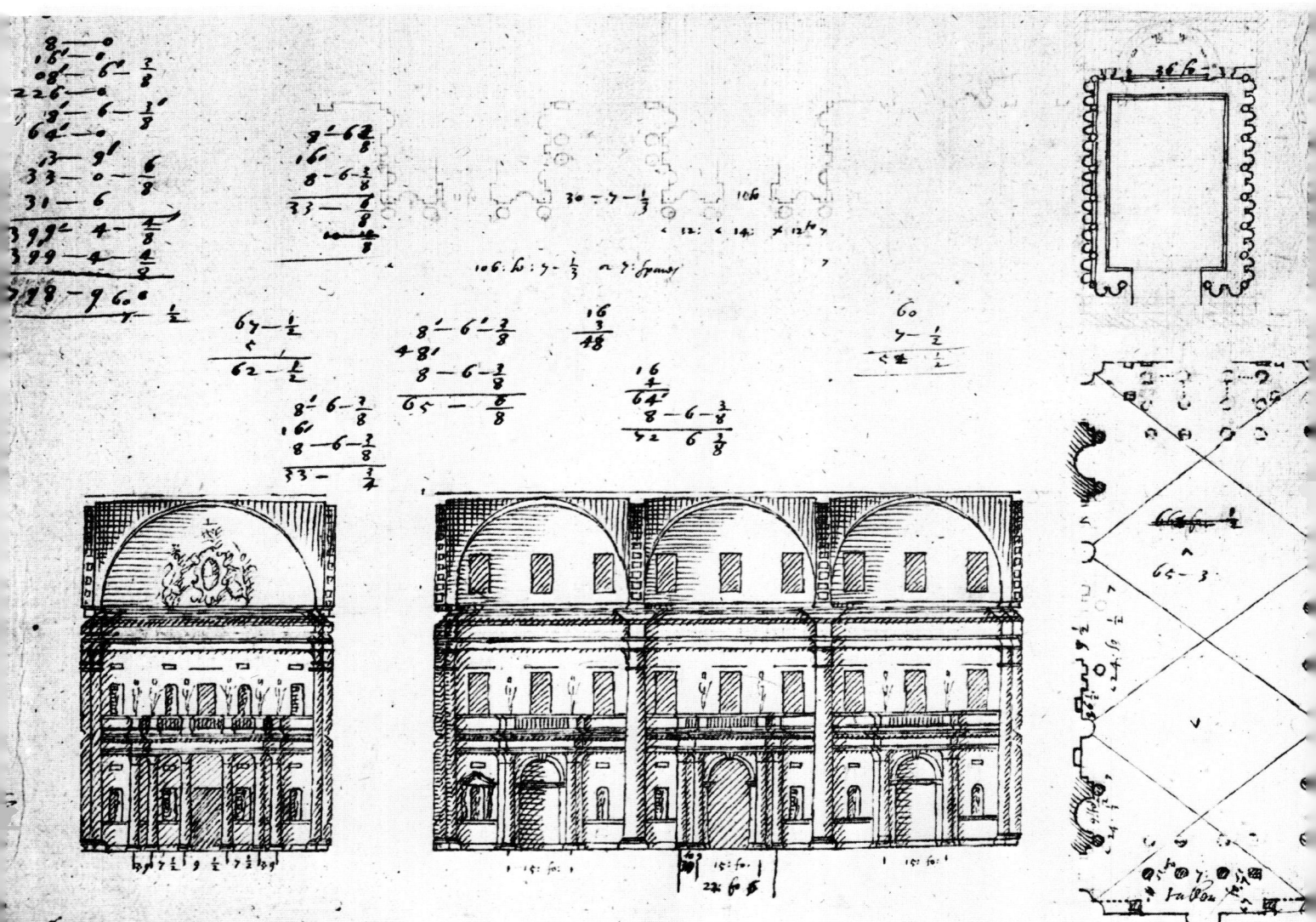

Plate 66 Inigo Jones and John Webb, Great Hall, Whitehall Palace project, interior elevations and plan extracted from larger drawings. (Devonshire Collections, Chatsworth, reproduced by permission of the Trustees of the Chatsworth Settlement from a photograph provided by the Courtauld Institute of Art, University of London.)

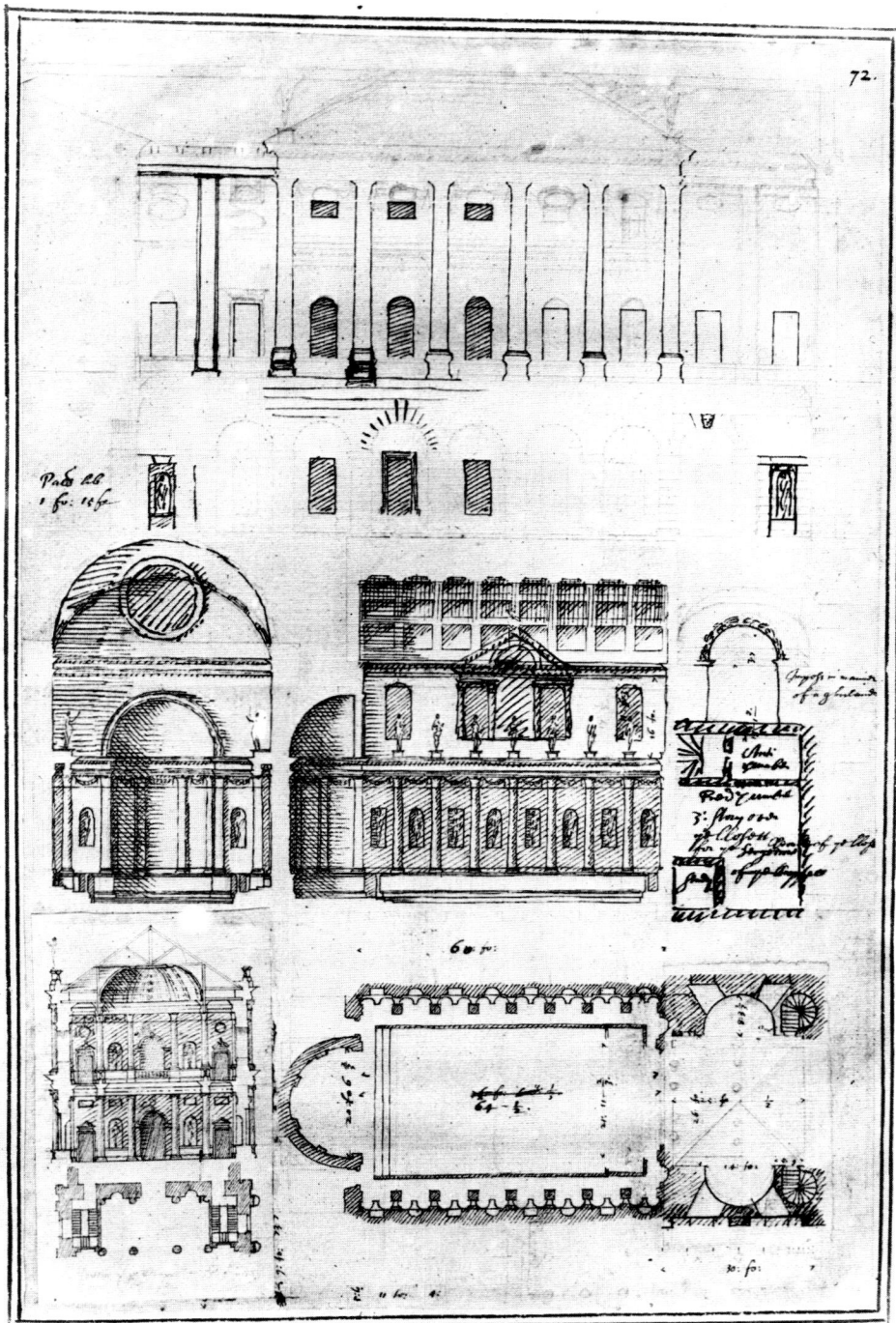

Plate 67 Inigo Jones and John Webb, Council Chamber, Whitehall Palace project, elevations and plan. (Devonshire Collections, Chatsworth, reproduced by permission of the Trustees of the Chatsworth Settlement from a photograph provided by the Courtauld Institute of Art, University of London.)

Plate 68   Inigo Jones and John Webb, Chapel, Whitehall Palace project, interior elevation and plan. (Devonshire Collections, Chatsworth, reproduced by permission of the Trustees of the Chatsworth Settlement from a photograph provided by the Courtauld Institute of Art, University of London.)

Plate 69 Juan de Herrera, Escorial, 1559–84, air view. (Anderson–Alinari.)

Plate 70   *Pierre Lescot, Square Court, Louvre, begun 1546. (Alinari.)*

Plate 71   Inigo Jones, The Queen's House, Greenwich (1616-35), from the south. (Photo: A. F. Kersting)

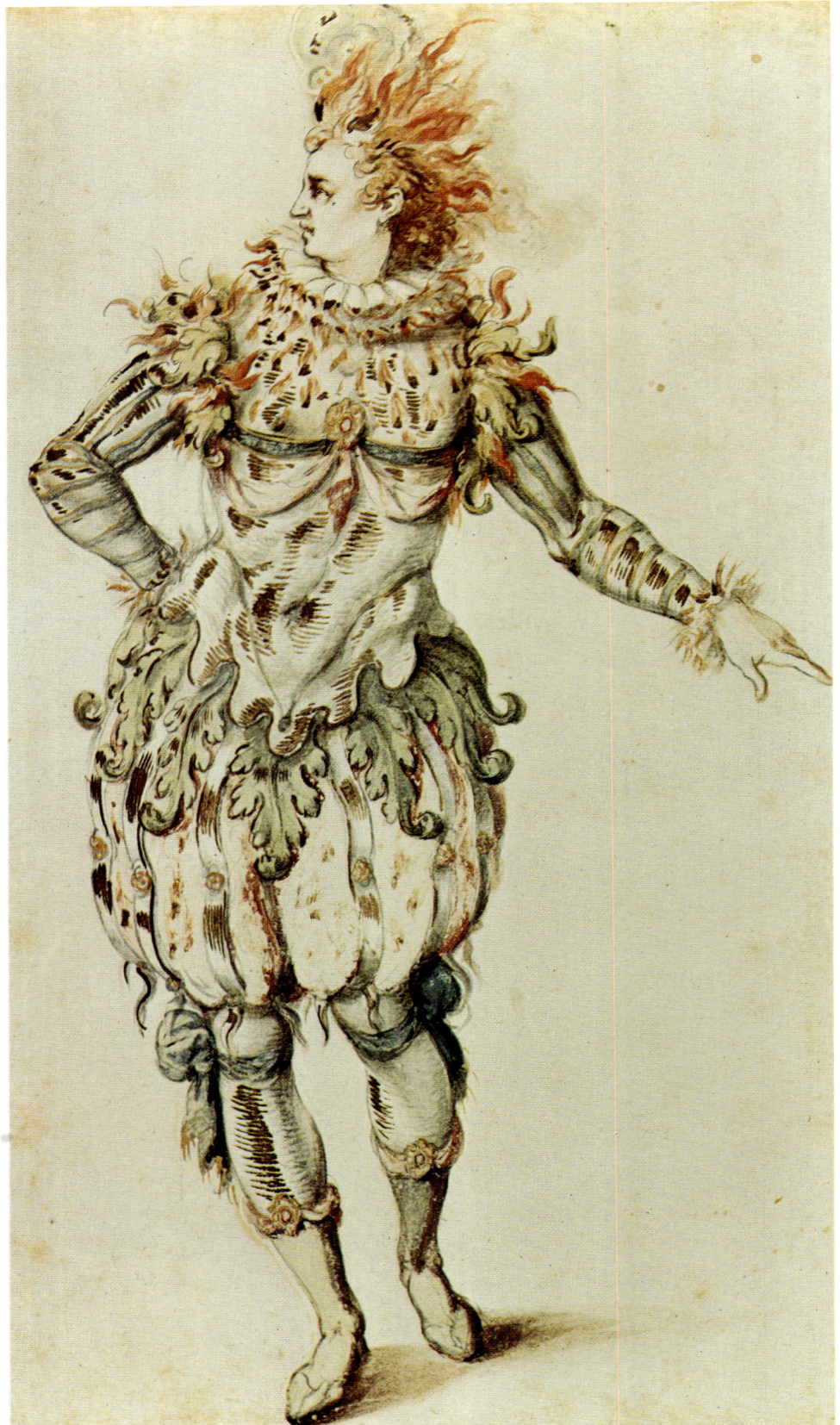

Plate 72 Inigo Jones, Masquer Lord: a Star, from The Lord's Masque, *1613. (Devonshire Collections, Chatsworth, reproduced by permission of the Trustees of the Chatsworth Settlement)*

Plate 73 Inigo Jones, Winged Masquer, from unknown masque c. 1605. (Devonshire Collections, Chatsworth, reproduced by permission of the Trustees of the Chatsworth Settlement)

Plate 74   Inigo Jones, Banqueting House, Whitehall. Exterior. (Photo: Mike Levers)

Plate 75   Inigo Jones, Banqueting House, Whitehall. Interior. (Photo: A. F. Kersting)

Plate 76 Inigo Jones, Queen's Chapel, St James's. Interior. (Reproduced by gracious permission of Her Majesty the Queen)